Tortoise, Tree Snake, Gator, and Sea Snake

For my friends at St. Christopher
School in Rocky River, Ohio
—B.P.C.

To Louis Gince. Wherever you are,
you are still the best pretend uncle.
—M.G.

Reptile:
an animal that has dry, scaly skin and breathes air with lungs

Tortoise, Tree Snake, Gator, and Sea Snake

What Is a Reptile?

by Brian P. Cleary

illustrations by Martin Goneau

Ⓜ Millbrook Press • Minneapolis

A **reptile** is an animal
with dry and scaly skin,

which serves to help protect it
while holding moisture in.

Reptiles all have backbones, so they're known as vertebrates.

6

This feature's one of many
on a list of reptile traits.

Although they're called cold-blooded, their blood's not always cold.

It means their bodies' temperature is outside their control.

Unlike us, their body heat
depends on what's around them.
They can be warm . . .

or hot . . .

or cool.

Depends on what surrounds them!

Unlike a young amphibian, a **reptile's** born with lungs.

And some don't use their nose to smell—
instead, they use their tongues!

When snakes and lizards stick their tongues out, they're not being rude.

Hee Hee

They're capturing small bits of scent.
This helps them hunt for food.

A **reptile** may eat many things
for health and strength and growth.

Some eat meat, and some eat plants, while others will eat both!

Some will dine on tiny bugs—

a spider,

ant,

or fly—

or even on the eggs that
other animals supply.

All **reptiles** breathe the air,

and most lay eggs on land.

They're found in oceans, deserts, plains, on grasses, dirt, and sand.

Many call the water home,
Like alligators,

snakes,

and crocodiles seen in marshes, rivers, swamps, and lakes.

Turtles live throughout the world, except where it's too cold.

They're found on land or sea or both and grow to be quite old.

Earth is home to many species,
and if you would span it,

You'd find 8,000 different kinds of **reptiles** on the planet!

Some will slither, some can walk,
while others
swim or crawl.

Most of them have shorter legs

(if they have legs at all!).

Lizards and turtles
and boas! (Oh my!)
Gators and geckos galore!

To boost your "rep" for **reptile** smarts, can you name even more?

So what is a **reptile**?
Do you know?

An animal is a reptile if . . .
- it has dry, scaly skin;
- it breathes air.

In addition, all reptiles . . .

- have a backbone (they're vertebrates);
- are born with lungs, unlike most baby amphibians;
- are cold-blooded animals. This means they cannot make their own body heat. Their bodies are the same temperature as their surroundings.

And most reptiles . . .

- lay hard-shelled eggs on land;
- live in warm places;
- have short legs or no legs and long tails;
- eat insects or other animals. (They're carnivores.) Some eat plants. (They're herbivores.) And some eat both plants and other animals. (They're omnivores.)

Find activities, games, and more at
www.brianpcleary.com

ABOUT THE AUTHOR & ILLUSTRATOR

BRIAN P. CLEARY is the author of the Words Are CATegorical®, Math Is CATegorical®, Adventures in Memory™, Sounds Like Reading®, and Food Is CATegorical™ series, as well as several picture books and poetry books. He lives in Cleveland, Ohio.

MARTIN GONEAU is the illustrator of the Food Is CATegorical™ series. He lives in Trois-Rivières, Québec.

Text copyright © 2013 by Brian P. Cleary
Illustrations copyright © 2013 by Lerner Publishing Group, Inc.

Millbrook Press
A division of Lerner Publishing Group, Inc.
241 First Avenue North
Minneapolis, MN 55401 U.S.A.

Website address: www.lernerbooks.com

Main body text set in Chauncy Decaf Medium 35/44. Typeface provided by the Chank Company.

Library of Congress Cataloging-in-Publication Data

Cleary, Brian P., 1959–
    Tortoise, Tree Snake, Gator, and Sea Snake : What Is a Reptile? / by Brian P. Cleary ; illustrated by Martin Goneau.
       p.   cm. — (Animal groups are CATegorical)
    ISBN: 978-0-7613-6210-4 (lib. bdg. : alk. paper)
    1. Reptiles—Juvenile literature. I. Goneau, Martin, ill. II. Title.
    QL644.2.C59 2013
    597.9—dc23   2011044869

Manufactured in the United States of America
1 – DP – 7/15/2012